Multiple Syndromes

Deadliest of sins, we corrupted our own
origins.

Surbhi

BookLeaf
Publishing

India | USA | UK

Made with ❤ on the BookLeaf Publishing Platform

www.bookleafpub.in

www.bookleafpub.com

Dedication

SCREAMING THE WORDS THAT YOU SWALLOWED
FOR TOO LONG

for the words buried in quiet
let them finally be heard

Preface

Poetry has always been a refuge for unspoken thoughts, a way to voice the emotions we suppress and the truths we dare not say aloud. Multiple Syndromes is born from that very space where words are not just written but felt, where emotions collide, and where silence finally finds its voice.

This collection is a reflection of the contradictions we live with, the sins we inherit, and the echoes of a past we can't escape. Every poem within these pages carries a piece of that struggle, an unfiltered expression of emotions too intense to be caged in whispers.

Being my first book, Multiple Syndromes is not just a collection of poems; it is a part of me. It holds the weight of words I once hesitated to write and the courage to finally let them exist. If these verses resonate with you, if they make you feel understood or even challenge you, then this book has found its purpose.

Let these words be a scream for those who have only known silence.

Acknowledgements

Writing *Multiple Syndromes* has been an emotional and transformative journey, one that wouldn't have been possible without the love, support, and encouragement of those around me.

First and foremost, I want to express my deepest gratitude to my parents for always believing in me and nurturing my creative spirit.
I want to thank my father for being a constant, tough pillar of support.
A special and profound thank you goes to my mother, who has always stood by me, whether in my best decisions or my most ridiculous ones. Their unwavering belief in me has given me the courage to chase every dream, no matter how uncertain or unconventional.

I also want to thank my friends, especially Shashank and Almas, for their constant support and inspiration. Shashank has been there every step of the way, cheering me on through every little success, while Almas has motivated me to write and always appreciated my efforts. Your combined belief in me has fueled my creative spirit and made this journey all the more rewarding.

To my readers, thank you for picking up this book, for allowing my words into your world. Whether you find solace, resonance, or even discomfort within these pages, I am grateful that you took the time to experience them.

Lastly, to every person who has inspired, challenged, or even doubted me, thank you. Each one of you, in your own way, has shaped the words within this book.

Love,
Surbhi

1. Pipe Dreams

I hate to admit, for what I see.
I'll pretend it ain't real, so let it be.
Screaming the words out loud,
But its ashes is all that comes to me,
And a whispered plea.
Cracks appear, illusions starts to fray.
I cling to mirage, refusing to sway.
They say,
"What's not yours is taken away."

Grasping at echoes of what could be,
Pipe dreams, refusing to see.
But when the smoke cleared,
All my fantasies seared.
Staring into the mirror, afraid to come home
Now I'm standing at your backdoor all alone.
No more shadows to deceive,
Only the bare truths, hard to believe.
Now as I can see,
Everyone looks better than me.

You got the best deals,

I'm still bargaining.
Up on the stage you are,
I'm down here dreaming.
The ocean blues melt at your feet,
I'm here longing for the rain.
Your crystals shimmer in bright sun,
While my pebbles just have stories spun.
For beauty lies in what we seek,
Maybe just in what others keep.

Doubts echo, but I'll deny.
The harsh reality, I'll defy.
You chase the moon,
I'll grasp the stars.
One wrong step, and falling back into the haze,
Pipe dreams, I'll still chase.

But all this chasing is making me go mad.
Indifference surrounds me,
It's making me sad.
You don't care about me?
Thanks, I'm glad.
But you know what's easier to assert?
It's to be angry than to tell you're hurt.

My heart, once sequined pink,
In the deep, dark ocean it sinks.
What if it's waiting for someone?
Someone to love me for who I am.
Now I just sit at the cold bottom,
Like an old skeleton with no blood left.
Pipe Dreams, an impossible theft.

This cold is cutting deep into my bone.
Please, I think it's enough.
Now, take me back home.
Where the sun shined,
Where all my poems rhymed.
You promised reality beyond the haze's veil,
But here I bleed, lost, beyond the pale.

So I'll just run,
Run far away,
Back into the haze,
'Cause it was always a safe place.
Mock me if you must, from your glittery shore,
It's easier when you haven't endured.
Running back into a burning house,

Just to save the things I love.
Is that self-love or self-destruction?
I don't know.
The one who decides is not me.
Pipe dreams, refusing to see.

2. Aurora Borealis

Every night, I prayed for the lights
That would light up my dull sky so bright,
In the shades of green,
With a hint of pink,
All my dreams in sync.

Every day, I dreamed of the aurora borealis,
And a sky full of stars,
A dream with scars.
Then one day, I saw your smile and your sparkling eyes,
Now I see it every night until the sunrise.
So it might just be you,
I dreamt of you,
It all seems so true.

Every evening, I saw in my mind
All the floating lights,
Lighting up my lost kingdom
With all the breathtaking sights.
Counting all the flowers in my braids,
Waiting for my life to begin.
It's been decades,

Just when you saw me,
I saw you,
And only you.

I woke up at 2 am,
With squinted and weary eyes,
To look for the shooting stars.
All the glittery sprinkles are falling like
The most beautiful meteor showers,
On you and me,
Just you and me.

It feels like a dream,
All the shades of green,
Lighting up my screen,
Shimmering like the moonbeam,
So, I'll say this to you,
That it's just you,
I dreamt of you,
It all feels so true.

3. Lullaby of Longing

Hand on the door handle,
For all I knew,
I paused to capture everything in my view,
Trying to sink it in,
But it'll be gone soon.
When I thought the faraway place was a treasure to win,
Now, it's all sinking in.

Cursing the vehicle that drove me away
From the place I wanted to leave,
From the place I loved,
From the place that felt like a cage,
From the place where I still longed to stay.
Landed in the city of dreams,
But I still dream of you.
Rhythm of hope in every beat,
But in every beat, I think of it.

Days of hoping, dreaming, and screaming,
Staring at the walls and the ceiling.
Need to clear space, memories to unpack,
So, I'll record it in writing as a backup track.

Seconds of sunshine, seconds of rain,
Maybe it was wiser to keep my feet on the ground and
stay sane,
Than to chase the illusions of the night sky.

The heart doesn't want something better;
It needs what it needs.
I thought here I would find hope, better ways, better
days,
But the place I left just says,
"I hope you find your dreams, wind in your wings,
And a lullaby that I'll sing,
Until you come back home again."

4. Who's been cruel to me?

I'm like a book with missing pages,
Slowly unfolding, without knowing,
Which page has been lost for ages.
I think I need healing,
But I don't know, what I need to heal on.
The naive, golden days,
I think they're all gone.

I'm trying to see the starry night,
With my hazy sight.
I longed to command the spotlight,
But I gripped onto fear, tighter than the microphone.
I profess not to mind, yet secretly,
All my thoughts are consumed by it.

Like a desert flower, I thirst for raindrops.
Yet I shrink away when they fall upon my petals.
I'm a moth drawn to flame,
Flame of attention,
Yet I flutter away when it comes too close.

I'm the thorns that adorn the rose,
Despising the pain they inflict,
Yet admiring the strength within.
I think I don't even remember,
The language my heart used to speak.

I speak of logic,
Yet I don't answer reason's call.
Who created all these huge walls?
How can you be anything,
If you even failed to be yourself?
Who stopped me from being myself?
I think it's me.

The ghosts I was scared of,
The monsters lurking in the shadows,
The devil in the space,
I think it has my face.

It was me who feared stepping on that stage.
It was me who thought maybe I couldn't pass the test.
It was me who stopped me from being my best.
So who's been cruel to me?
Than anyone else could ever be?

I think it's me.
I extinguished the flames,
'Cause it burned too gently.
Yet I craved for the gentle warmth.
Who's gonna stop me from crashing into flames?
If not me, then nobody can.

5. Always yet never again

How does it feel to be loved and not loved at all at the same time?

How does it feel to be bright but not bright enough to make them see at the same time?

How does it feel to be included and not included at all at the same time?

How does it feel to be wanted and not wanted at all at the same time?

How does it feel to be lively and a living corpse at the same time?

How does it feel to be shining and rusting at the same time?

How does it feel from being a home to a shelter for someone at the same time?

How does it feel to be able to speak but never heard at the same time?

How does it feel to be seen and ignored at the same time?

How does it feel to be present but never there at the same time?

How does it feel to be screaming yet no one could listen at the same time?

Always yet never again

6. The War

Blood dripping down my veins,
Wiped it on a white cloth,
The war was called off.
I kept my armor down.
Months of breathing fresh air,
But memories of the war kept me up till 2 am.
All the scar under my skin,
Sometimes it does hurt.

You opted for a truce,
I hid my sword behind the bush.
Maybe the past is the reason,
Screaming inside my head,
That's why I keep my guns close.
I would put you in a trial,
For the crimes you never did.

I couldn't fight anymore,
But the reflexes are so good,
One hint of betrayal,
I'll punch a hole
In the ice frozen ground,

Pull out my sword,
And call off the truce.

When you said
Darling,
Love is war,
It was never fair.
But, we could live in peace.
How I gave up all my shares
Hold my hand and we would never go back there.

7. Mr. Mafia

I was so lost in a dream,
Under the moonbeam
Woke up to this awful scene.
Splashing inks, ataraxia sinks.
Now I'm all blue, thanks to you.
It can't be a real thing,
But it is.
It's all coming down,
Someone stop this plangent sound.

Mr. Mafia,
Gleaming in his suit, all star-studded
Supercilious, pretentious but high-handed.
Glitter dusted on all his crimes,
Life is a circle, ticking times.
Round and round, the cycle spins,
How about catching up with your bad deeds,
Starting from where it begins ?

I chose to be quiet,
I hoped you'd discern,
But you'll never learn.

No more compliance,
So I chose to break my silence.
Your jewels used to shine so bright,
But I can see the fool's gold rusting in daylight.

Mr. Mafia,
Thinks he's the only one,
But his stupid stunts, they're already done.
He who won't ever be sorry,
no remorse in his story,
Always trying to prove that he's worthy,
Eternally chasing fleeting glory.
What about all the souls you tried to crush?
They're all now lifeless bodies.
With everything you got in your power,
You darkened their days,
turned them into wilted flowers.

I can see the things you do,
There's a reason you can't be nice all through,
Because people like them won't let you.
So now, I carry guns in my pocket,
Had enough, now, it's time to stop it.
They say, all this will make you strong,
But I had to pay the price,

For everything you did me wrong.

Mr. Mafia,
Whose shiny shore is selective.
You can be there only if you're his favorite kid.
Who's a demon that feeds on others' fears,
Just for some bits of popularity, it appears.
Who thinks he's above everyone else,
In his delusion, he dwells,
Pushes those who threaten his fake boundaries,
Curses them in his dark spells.

You cursed me, your taunt stings,
Wrath on my wings.
Now I'm mad,
And this is gonna be bad.
I tried to be an angel,
But, you won't let me,
Kept poking the devil in me.
So I'll curse you in a poem,
See how the realms bend,
As my hands write your dead end.
There's no point proving my worth,
As you'll always try to cut my name,
You'd be a fool if you believed people change.

Mr. Mafia,

Who tries to be sophisticated,

Doesn't accept he's a bit overrated.

Who thinks he's above everyone else,

Killing those who threatens his fake shells.

Who had all the stars studded in his expensive suits,

Yet still went after my pocketful of stars, proud of the

loot.

Darkness masked with all your shiny outfits,
Trying to block me with all your force and wits.
They proscribed you, yet you're still here,
Persisting in shadows, driven by fear.
I can't forgive, what I'll do is unforgivable,
'Cause you left me like this, feeling miserable.
This is one hell of a place,
Whoever comes here gets lost in this space.

Mr. Mafia,

Who tries to crush others, in a bid to ascend,

Playing a game he doesn't comprehend.

Thinking he could win it, but I see better,

With so many choices, he picked the worst, I fear.

Sanity won't fix it.
Need to lose it to mend this.
Over is this game of chess,
Now pack up all your stuff,

It's time to clean this mess.
With faith tossed, bridges lost,
This is what it cost.
Do what you're good in,
Show me who you really are.

                    Mr. Mafia,
                  Whose suit and tie,
                Were too good to hide,
               The pettiest man inside.
              Who branded me as deceitful,
                I'll acknowledge it as fact.
            So who's the one good in this act?
          With all his gold, infinite to choose,
         Nothing to gain, everything to lose.

8. My gold rusts without my touch

Cursing you for
Every lie you spoke,
Every false hope you built.
Void lingers in my eyes,
I trusted you like a child
Unaware of the knife you hid behind your back.
Never thought I'd do this,
But I'll kill you in every verse I write.

You stole my words,
Used my verses for your gain.
I didn't know you'd leave me bleeding,
But I see now
You'll trap a hundred more, mocking their pain.
Stab me once, stab me twice;
My words will still haunt you each night.

Little did you know,
Burying me would leave you cursed,
The echoes of betrayal will find their way back,
For my gold rusts without my touch,

My stories that you stole will be your worst nightmare.
Every time you killed me will kill you just as deep.
And every tear that falls from my eyes
Will drown you in a sea of your own despair.
I hope you never forget that.

9. If you ever get lost, get lost with me

I can't hide it in my mind anymore,
Not when I can see it all.
You know how scared I am of heights
Being at the top of the world
Seems like a very long fall.
I know you know it too.

You smile like everything's fine,
But the screams in your head remain unheard.
I'll scream them for you,
Until I have no voice left
To even whisper your name.
Will you still hear me?

Their quixotic code of honor,
And then they fled the scene.
We've been so broken ever since,
But I'm glad we share the pain.
You jumped off the cliff
Before I had a chance to save you.
Tell me, what is it

That I failed to give you all this time?

But I'll be jumping after you,
I'll save you no matter what.
Saving you will save me,
What doesn't kill you now
Will kill you eventually.
You know I know this too.
I know how scared you are of having wings
That might weigh you down.

Funny isn't it,
How a soul departing can bring everyone together,
Yet none when it stays.
Please don't leave, don't leave me.
I'm not much, but I'm all I have.
I don't know where I lost all the sunshine,
When they cut the trees,
Burned the whole forest down.
I'm still standing there trying to get somewhere,
Somewhere even I don't know.

They're so rich when it comes to the currency of cruelty,
We can go nowhere with what we have.

And you know how scared I am of my prayers going
unheard,
But every night, I still pray for the light.
So if you ever get lost, get lost with me.
Make me your shelter until you find your home.

10. Cried until I died

Back then, did you know
All your dreams would turn to dust?
Did the little kid within you know
That your life would be a compromise, again and again?
Did the light in you foresee
You'd have to keep searching for hope when there's none
to find?

If I were you,
I think I would've cried until I died,
Unable to find a reason to paste a smile.
But I want you to know,
Even if everything around you feels rusted,
To me,
You'll always be the one who sparkles eternally.
To me,
You'll always be the god I'll worship forever.

11. Ask Me To Stay

You say this is how it's supposed to be,
And I say maybe.
We thought it would be a matter of time,
But maybe it's not.

I remember when this place felt known,
Because we called it ours,
we called it home.

Now I glance back for one last sight,
Can we return, or is it goodbye tonight?
You know I left a part of me in that space,
Just to forever haunt that place.

Stop and look back.
Stop and stay back.
Stop and hold back.

Every day I stare at the new place with oceans in my
eyes.
How can they say it's gonna be alright?

I didn't sleep the whole night and tried to give you
signals,
I paced the room the whole night,
But you said it's gonna be alright.

Lifeless hues covered the whole place.
I tried to tell you,
That we were running out of time.

And I know my hurt is an unfair demand
On everyone I care about.
So now I'm stepping down the stage,
Still wishing I could turn back and take it all in.

Stop me and ask me to look back.
Stop me and ask me to hold on.
Stop me and ask me to stay.

Lifelong, this place would sing a sad song,
As we are too far gone
To be able to return.

But I'd run back to that place
If you'd call my name,
If you'd feel the same.
If you'd ask me to stay.

Until then, I've got nothing to hold on to
Unless you say you choose me.

12. The dead tell no tales

Pitch-black horizon, raging skies,
Fell off the cliff, lost in the tides,
Swallowed by the night,
Drowning in the indigo,
Emerging from uncertainty,
Holding on to not let go,
Found a home nearby.

You were a sanctuary,
And I lingered at its gates.
I saw you in peace,
With me standing outside.
But, I still knocked on your door,
Wondering if what i did was right.

I can see it all,
I notice every single thing you do,
Standing here from afar,
Watching everything in my view.

You said you regret it,

Windows shattered as the storm hit,
And how I still tried to fix it,
But when I couldn't,
I spent love for every broken piece,
Blood dripping out the veins,
Engulfed in all this pain.

I made you my favorite book,
But you left me in the draft,
Collecting every word you spoke,
Even if it's the heart that it broke.
Silenced every word I spoke.

Now I'm trying to make some sense of everything that's
gone,
Love that left to mourn.
I left and you watched me leave,
Didn't even asked me to stay,
Could a different road lead to a better way?

But I still miss your smile,
Standing in exile,
I wish you'd hear me out,
Silence screaming, love sinking,

High in delusion, love's an illusion.

What must it be like to be the priority?
What must it be like to get everything you want,
Without ever bleeding for it?
What would it be like to have the perfect frames,
Without ever trying to fix the broken pieces?
Should I still dare to ask?

Lights twinkling,
Warm and sparkling,
I stand outside,
Almost knocked on your door.
We're on the last page,
Nothing more to unfold,
For the dead tell no tales,
Their stories untold.

13. My man's a satan's spawn

His eyes like stars, yet cold as winter's night,
Oh, what a diabolic delight.
His smile has made tons of victims to his game,
A tempting devil cloaked in human frame.
With every word, my senses reel and spin,
Even when you know you can't win.
He plays along, like a devil in disguise,
Feeding the flames that burn within my eyes.

They don't understand me
When I say
My obsession's bone-deep.
I couldn't get away from him.
These feelings don't have brakes for him,
Killing me enough to keep me alive.
And they told me not to lose my mind,
Even if it's something bad,
It's still something I wanna have.

Summer air, street lights glow,
Rain splashing on the windows,

You throw your jacket on the floor,
I memorize these scenes heart-core.
All these worldly glories
Compare to nothing compared to you.
You make me feel like the world is ours,
Even if your love is so cruel,
It's forgiven as I'm a fool,
'Cause in love they say, there's no rule.

I still believe in your false love.
Hell is when you're away,
But it's a hellish heaven when you stay.
Poet of deception, craft me in your verses of charm,
Sculpting chaos, molding it into artistry.
I still weave your fantasies,
Despite the jagged edges of your betrayal.

I'm not the one to blame,
This Mephistophelian model made me insane.
I could lose a hundred times,
If you're the one playing along,
Trading my halo for shadows,
For you I'd forsake my celestial throne,
Willingly descending from heavens,
'Cause my man's a satan's spawn.

Infernal idol,
Scheming Machiavel,
Oh Lord, save me,
But at least he could burn the world for me.

This obsession, this addiction,
It's making me want you even more.
Blind love is a crazy thing.
I hate what's forbidden,
Deadliest of sins,
We corrupted our own origins,
Now even if we get burned,
At least it was an eternal fire,
Oh, these never-ending desires.

14. Which god should I pray to for you?

When they confirmed our fear,
I never told you I was scared.
Each night, I cried myself to sleep,
Each night, I stayed up late
Just to look at your face.

Maybe I can't pretend for long,
Maybe I'm not strong enough.
I break down every time I think about it.
You don't know how much I fear
That my prayers would go unheard.
Maybe that's why I never ask for what I want.

I know when someone is pretending
I do it every time just not to let that hope die.
But I'd bargain everything I have if it's for you.
I'd believe in everything you believe if it's for you.
Tell me, which god should I pray to for you?

I hate to see you in pain,
And I hate it even more when I can't help it.
I know it's difficult for you,
But I can't do anything without you.

When she told me maybe I could lose you,
I broke down on my way back home.
I couldn't even hide in plain sight.
I thought about it that very night
Without you, I might just die.

> What would everything I ever do be for?
> Who would call my name?
> Who would be there for me?
> Who would my eyes look for?

Every word would be meaningless.
What am I supposed to say?
What am I supposed to write?
The only thing I can do is beg
Stay with me, or take me with you.
Don't leave me stranded in a world without you.

15. Twisting minds with a nod

I forgot how it felt to be happy all the time,
All of this weight, and always out of line.
Weeping through nights that stretched on for months,
While those who say they love, never care as much.
They claim that they care, but it's all just a lie,
Leaving you wondering why you even try.
Those who surrounds, they hide it so well,
But deep down, they don't mean what they tell.

They say I'm never in my senses,
Lost in my mind, jumping over these fences.
Maybe I'm just trapped behind my defenses.
But still always out of control
Let me confess something
I'm the poison in your way,
Praying for an easy end to your day.
Walking around the grave,
Watching you leave,
Witnessing the end of all your deeds.

Thinking they know the best of me,

Or maybe just the worst they see.
Interested in my love track ?
How about giving a little respect back?
And I get to write your path
Like the death note
With the pen that hell gave me,
Time to let it go, set you free.
So I'll take it to the grave,
Walk around and watch you fade.

When they warned I serve poison dusted with glitter,
You should have caught the clues, harsh and bitter.
Noticed the signs I gave,
Now you're trapped in the mess you made.
I try to stay invisible, away from light,
But you always drag me into the fight.

So now take a look into my palace,
The diamonds all covered in dust and malice.
With darkness around,
No light to be found,
You wouldn't dare to step on this ground.
Yes I'm wrong and flawed,
Twisting minds with a nod.
Could you step in?

Would you step in?

Mirror, mirror,
Who's the most pretentious of them all?
I can't see my reflection

Maybe, you should go and take a look into the mirror.

16. You've always been mine

You're there in my sweetest dreams,
I see you everywhere.
A list of reasons why I should stop thinking about you
Yet, I never do.

Are you even real, or just a trick of my imagination?
But if you ever show up, how would I know it's you?
Or maybe I would.
I see this one place where I know I'll find you
I just need to reach it.
You stole my heart long ago,
I don't have it to give to anyone else.

Why do you think I'll be fine without you?
I'm not.
Just come to me,
I'll forever run to you.
Nobody is like you
I never found anyone else, or maybe I was never looking.
It's you.
Only you.

Sometimes I wonder if you'll ever step out of my head.
It's driving me crazy.
Tell me, does it bother you?
They don't understand me like you do.
All my letters are addressed to you,
Written in invisible ink.

They might try to take your place,
But what they don't know
That place belongs to you.
In a room full of people,
My eyes search only for you.
You're the best thing I have,
Even if only in my mind.
I'd choose you over anyone, every time.
Because you've always been mine.

17. R.E.S.T

The rain
I know it's gone.
But every time it rains,
Do you miss me?

> The escape
> I know I never said goodbye.
> Do you still hate me?

The smoke
I know that's us,
Disappearing just like that.

> The unspoken truths
> I know the damaged I caused.
> Did you cursed me?

18. Reminisce, Forfeit, Oblivion

You left all the love here in this hall,
inside the walls of my phenomenally stupid heart.
I hoped for your choice, but it never came.
Down to dust, the love set aflame.

Screams that don't exist loud enough to make you listen,
Fire that gives no warmth, only smoke.
Numb, cold, empty vision.
Hopes no longer evoke.

Even if I give it away?
This love's gonna curse me anyway.
What if your love made me weaker,
weaker than I ever was?

If my suffering is your priority,
and if it's all you want from me,
then let me tell you
how your silence has killed me
in the most brutal way possible.

I dream of a place,
sitting on the grave,
where we can understand the language
of what they call love.

This love,
a rainstorm that only soaks the heart, not the soil.
So tell me, where is this love supposed to go?
Where is the man I used to know?

The more you reminisce,
the more you forfeit,
the more it slips into oblivion.

19. What a way to die

My love was so cruel but some wanted to be destroyed.
My boy was a work of art,
I ruined the craft and left it in the backyard.

I jumped into the ocean, drowning in the blues,
For him it's everyday.
He was a breath of fresh air,
but now he breathes smoke.

Sometimes we don't know
what do we need exactly,
Locked in the drawers are the apologies,
That you never heard and I never said.

Love is the water that can either
carry you to heaven or pull you under,
Either way you have to surrender.
Either way you lose.
Lifting you high,
Oh, what a way to die.

20. Trying to get somewhere

Don't know where I lost the sunshine
Clouds covered the sky,
And I didn't even realize
Until all the light was gone.

They ask me, "What's wrong with you?"
"Why don't you talk much?"
But hey,
This is just how it is now.

You can find me in all of my poems,
Always drowning in my own hell.

I knew this street like the back of my hand,
But suddenly, I couldn't find my way.
I knew the soil like a part of my soul,
But now it's nowhere to be found.

Like the old tree they chopped down
The one where we used to play.
Just for a minute,
Take me back to that moment
I need to make some sense of it all.

When they chopped down the trees,
Burned the forest to the ground,
And went back to their homes,
Leaving me alone

I'm still on that roadway,
And I still don't know why.
But I'm still trying to get somewhere
Somewhere even I don't remember.

21. It kills you eventually

I know what happens next
I've written this scene many times.
It all ends right then and there,
So I'll step right out of this script.

> You never even tried to hear my story,
> Never tried to understand my words.
> So I'll walk away, and I know
> You'll just watch me leave.

When the heart breaks,
It never makes a sound,
But it kills you
If not now, then eventually.

> I still remember the rain, your smile,
> And how you were shaking.
> I closed the windows for you,
> But now they suffocate me.

What do you do now?
Laugh at me?
Pity me?

Do you know what I do?
I skip all your favorite songs.
I hate that place where I still see us.
I hope forgetting you haunts you.
I wish I could curse you
And I mean it.

I'll erase every file of us,
Throw away every belonging
That reminds me of you.

With every drop of ink
That bleeds from my veins,
I hope it stains every single one of your blank pages
Just so what doesn't kill you now
Kills you eventually.

www.ingramcontent.com/pod-product-compliance
Lightning Source LLC
LaVergne TN
LVHW021247200726

843509LV00012B/1600